From a Caterpillar to a Butterfly

a novel

Tanisha Danyette Brandon

Outskirts Press, Inc.
Denver, Colorado

This book is dedicated to my parents who have always believed in me, my husband who has always encouraged me, my kids for inspiring me, H.U.M.B.L.E Beginnings for holding me accountable, and to my brother LaVel. May you rest in peace. Putting my MGP (Multi Game Plan) in play for you! Here's to many more dreams being accomplished! ~TBF

Chapter One

"The garage door! Open the garage door!" Mom was yelling and I had yet to hear her.

A few moments later, she stepped into the kitchen. She threw a deadly glare in my direction. "Minah! I have been calling you for the last five minutes. What are you doing in here?"

I turned around to look at my mother. I had been studying math with my headphones on, as usual. At 5'10", she was a tall, slender woman. She was also beautiful. Mom used to be a model, but right now the only thing she was modeling was a look of a serial killer. Plus her arms were filled with grocery bags, so I knew she was not happy.

I took the headphones off and stood up, preparing to walk to her. "I'm sorry, Mom. I guess I spaced out. Do you still need me?"

"Forget it. I got it myself," She sat the bags down on

the kitchen counter, plopped in a chair and patted her French twist. For two years I have been trying to get my hair like that, and I still can't. She turned her attention towards me. "So, how was your day?" She was cheerful again. Mom has mood swings like you wouldn't believe.

I gulped. "Awful," I tugged at my bun- my current hairstyle. "Mrs. Jackson gave back the book reports today, and I got a C. I know I deserved more than that so..."

Mom sighed deeply. "Um, excuse me dear, but . . . well, I know I said I wouldn't bother you about this, but Minah sweetheart, have you given any thought to your Valentine's dance?"

I looked at her in surprise. She had totally caught me off guard.

"Mom, I really don't see much point in discussing the dance, since I don't have a valentine, and I don't see any prospects in the future."

"Well, have you asked around? I remember when you would just walk up to a young man and dazzle him with your smile. I'm sure there are some guys out there that would die to take you to that dance." Mom smiled.

I shook my head sadly. "Mom, I seriously doubt that. Besides, I just do not have any interest in dating. I'd rather get good grades and get into a good college."

"Oh my goodness, not that old line again," Mom took a deep breath. "Minah, I understand what you're saying. And you know I encourage you to make school a priority, work hard and get good grades, but you have *already* been accepted into a very good college! I mean, you can't do much better than Spelman, and your grades are good-- 4.0 I might add. You are a *senior* in high school. In a few months, you'll be graduating. You can breathe now. No pressure. Just relax a bit."

Mom walked over and put her hands on my face to force me to look at her. "I'm worried about you. It doesn't seem right for a pretty girl like you to be cooped up in the house every Friday and Saturday night."

I gently took Mom's hands off of my face and started unpacking the grocery bags. "I'm not cooped up in the house every weekend. Amity and I go out sometimes. I mean when she's not on the phone with Justin. I just don't see why…"

"Minah look," Mom took a final deep breath and appeared to be counting backwards, but I couldn't be sure. She stood up and began to put the dishes away. "Ever since you and Patrick broke up, you haven't even wanted to talk to other guys. It's been a year. Sweetie, it's your last year in high school. I just want you to enjoy it." She glanced at me.

"Well, I'm going to Grad Nite, the Senior Trip, and hopefully the Senior Ball. I do plan to enjoy the year," I got up and walked to the refrigerator. "Now what should we have for dinner?"

"It's hopeless," Mom sighed. She closed the cabinet and walked over to me. "Just don't waste the rest of this year with your nose in the books all the time, or you may look up and find that all the fun has passed you by."

"Don't worry Mom. Now how about turkey breast and potatoes for dinner?" I looked at her questioningly.

"Umm, no potatoes. I'm on a diet. Better make it a salad."

I resisted the urge to roll my eyes. Mom is always on a diet. She owns a successful fashion design company and likes to stay fit for the business. It's pretty easy for her, she naturally eats healthy and likes to exercise, but occasionally a few pounds sneak up on her. In her business, that's not a good thing. Tell me, where did people get the idea that a size 6 was not a "good" fit? The runway is filled with models that look like sticks. I want to look at someone who looks like me. Size 10 and happy!

Okay, enough of my soapbox.

We started dinner, me with the turkey breast, Mom with the salad. This was always the best time for our mother/daughter chats. I know it probably seems like Mom and I don't get along, but she's my best friend, and right now she's worried about me. I've tried to hide it, but I'm worried too. My last boyfriend Patrick and I were together for two years. We met freshman year. We were like magnets drawn to each other, had everything in common. Then, junior year, I caught him cheating on me with Erika Bowen, the school slut. I was more than mad; I was furious and really hurt! It seems like now I can't meet a guy I can trust. I don't want to get hurt again.

So for now I am avoiding all guys. The best way to do that is to study till I drop. And basically that's what I do. I only go out when my best friend Amity drags me. Mom is always on my case, but frankly I've decided the best thing for me to do is stay away from guys. They are nothing but trouble. Eventually I'll find a good one, but until then I'll just keep busy with school. The only problem is that my life used to be way more than school. I was part of the drama club, had run for student government and even donated my painting skills to the local nursing home. Actually, come to think of it, I haven't even visited the home since my break up with Patrick. What has happened to me?

After dinner, Mom and I headed to our "PSP's" or personal space places. For Mom that meant changing into her black silk kimono and lying on the couch in front of the TV. For me that meant going up to my room and taking out my school books to study.

I really should describe my room to you. It's always a surprise to people who have never seen it. Like I said before, I'm a quiet person and basically stay home a lot, so I wanted my room to be a place where I would always love to be. It is! My room is too special, if I can brag on myself a bit. The inspiration is my favorite colored pillow. It is teal with black tassels. It has always been my favorite pillow, and I saw the colors and went wild with my room. I was able to convince Mom to get a teal carpet, and it actually came out pretty nice. I have a black wicker headboard, teal and black comforter and a matching wicker love seat with my precious pillow as the centerpiece. I painted a mural of a teal sun with black highlights on my wall and have striped curtains to compliment the room.

The reason people are shocked when they see my room is because looking at me, you would think I had not a drop of creative style. Since the breakup I started dressing very simply. The same outfit of jeans and t-shirts is my daily uniform. It made shopping easy and it fit my mood. I didn't want anyone to notice me- any guys, that is. So I went from wearing my shoulder length wavy hair loose, to wearing it in a tight bun. Went from stylish outfits to simple jeans and t-shirts, went from pricey perfume to basic bar soap. I guess it worked because I haven't been bothered by guys in a long time. I guess that's what I wanted. But sometimes when I answer the phone, I wish it was a cute guy asking me out instead of one of Mom's clients or Amity. Well, I made my decision, and now I have to stick to it. Don't I?

Chapter Two

"Hey Minah, can we join you guys?"

Amity and I looked up at the voice. We were in the school cafeteria and had been discussing her latest problems with her boyfriend, Justin. Frankly I was happy for the interruption. Amity has been my best friend forever. We basically shared pacifiers. We even resemble each other. She is the closest thing I have to a sister, but her boyfriend Justin is a topic of conversation I tire of easily.

"Sure. Sit down." We moved to give them room.

Anthony, Ben and Jeremy were among the cutest guys in school. At one time or another almost all of the girls had a crush on them. We all grew up together with the exception of Jeremy. Me, Anthony, Ben and Amity used to have a club called Four Pals. When we got into seventh grade, the club just kinda ended, but we still hang out a lot. Jeremy had just moved to the San Jose area a few months ago, but he already had a huge fan club. He claims up and down that in Georgia the girls never paid attention to him. When I first heard that, I laughed and told him it must be the California water. I can see why Jeremy has such a huge following. Jeremy is beyond cute; he is almost god-like. With his black wavy hair, his sexy dark brown eyes, and pretty straight almost boyish smile, not to mention an almost perfect body (Jeremy works out regularly) he made me do a double-take sometimes. The neat thing about Jeremy is that he's not conceited. In fact he's pretty modest. That's one reason we all like him.

"So what are you two up to today?" Anthony was asking us. He picked up his sandwich and took a huge bite. His brown eyes twinkled. Anthony has a baby face with smooth brown skin.

"Oh you know, the same junk. School, gossip, homework, and sleep," I answered. I rolled my eyes at Amity.

"Could your life be any more boring?" Ben asked me.

Then I rolled my eyes at *him*. "I don't consider it boring, thank you," I picked up a french fry off of his tray. "Besides, it's better than hanging around watching videos like you dorks do."

"Yeah," Amity chimed in. "And anyway, who are you to say someone's life is boring? Personally I like to go out once in awhile, but if Minah chooses to stay in her room 24/7, that's her business. Right, Minah?"

I gave her a look. "Yeah, thanks," I said wryly.

"Minah, we're all going to the movies tonight. Want to come?" Jeremy looked into my eyes with concern.

I began to answer and he cut me off.

"And don't say you have homework-- it's Friday. You can do it on Saturday or even *Sunday*" Jeremy gasped playfully.

I looked around. Everyone was waiting for my answer. I shrugged my shoulders. "Alright. Sure, I'll go."

"You will?" Amity seemed surprised. She actually

leaned close to my face.

I leaned back frowning. "Well, I'm not a hermit, for God's sake."

"You live like one though," Ben argued.

"Well I'm going to the movie. Isn't that enough? Aren't you happy?" I looked around the table at the faces of my friends.

Amity shrugged her shoulders. "Yeah, I guess so."

Anthony shook his head. "Will wonders never cease?" he muttered.

"Good. Then it's settled." I went back to eating my sandwich and tried to hide my smile.

Chapter Three

A few weeks later, news about the school play came up. It was a way for the seniors to say goodbye to the school with a dramatic flair. The cast would consist of only seniors, and all were encouraged to join in. The senior advisor had written the play himself, and although all seniors were automatically part of the cast, he wanted auditions for the lead roles. I surprised both myself and Amity when I decided to go for one of the leading roles.

"What? You're actually going to audition?" she exclaimed.

"I happen to be a pretty good actress," I gave her an indignant look. "I was the leading lady in Othello *and* Grease, remember!"

"Of course I remember," She gave me an exasperated sigh. "I went to all of the performances. I'm just shocked. I mean back then you were really into being the center of attention. You were social, going out all of the time…"

"Look Amity. You're my best friend so I'm going to tell you this," I took a deep breath. "I'm human too…"

"I know that," Amity cut in impatiently.

"No. I mean, well, I have been living so crazy for the past year that I almost feel trapped by it. I don't know how I got to this point. I mean, who am I anymore? I want to get out there before it's too late. But I've already forgotten the simplest stuff. Like talking to guys, doing my hair. What everyone is wearing. What's happening at school or in the community. I mean those things were huge in getting accepted to Spelman, but they were also really important to who I was, I mean am. I've spent so much time in my books that I haven't taken any time to look around. Mom's right. I'm going to let my senior year slip by, and not have any fun to show for it. I thought trying out for the play might help." I looked at her desperately.

"Minah relax," she said. "You're on the right track. It's all going to come back to you. It's like learning to ride a bike. You never forget how."

"That's why I love you," I hugged her. "You say the most ridiculous things and they always make sense."

She looked at me and slowly started to laugh. I hugged her even harder and laughed right along with her.

"Look, I need you. I love you. I've always loved you."

"Stop. Stop. Stop."

I looked at the director, Mr. Green. "What's wrong this time?" I asked. We had done the same scene six times already and he always stopped me at the same point.

"Minah, you're fine until you get to the word love," he paused for a second. "But then you're not convincing. How am I supposed to believe that this is the man you fell in love with three years ago and have been following around ever since?"

I had no idea. This script wasn't the masterpiece I had

hoped for, but it would do, even if it was a little on the corny side.

"I don't know," I said aloud. "What do you suggest?" I tried hard not to roll my eyes.

"I'm giving you homework," Mr. Green informed me. "You are to say 'I love you' at least five times a day to yourself until you sound convincing to everyone."

"Are you serious?" I looked around at the rest of the cast. "It can't be that bad." Everyone avoided my eyes. "Is this a joke?"

"Not unless you take this role as a joke," Mr. Green said seriously. "This may not be the best play, but you're a good actress, you can convince the audience it is. You have to feel the part or you're only going to hurt it. Understand? Oh, and I want you to work with the understudy for Jason's role."

I really respected Mr. Green. He had directed the last play I was in and he was always able to bring the best out of me. I knew he was only trying to help. I felt I owed it to him to at least listen. The only part I wasn't excited about was Jason, my leading man. Jason Campbell was a grade A jerk. The only thing he had in his favor was a gorgeous body, beautiful eyes, a beautiful face, and a beautiful voice. Unfortunately he also had a gigantic beautiful ego to go with it. He was extremely conceited. He was playing the opposite leading role and unlike me, he was having no problems during our morning rehearsals. But, because of Jason's busy schedule- he played baseball-he was unable to rehearse after school hours, so I would be forced to work with the understudy .I had no idea who he was since the understudies had not yet started coming to rehearsals.

"I'm going to give the understudy your address and you can expect a visit this afternoon," Mr. Green paused and looked up. "Oh, is that alright?"

I got the point right away. I had no choice. "Yeah, sure. Oh, Mr. Green, who is the understudy anyway?"

But Mr. Green had already started walking down the stage steps and out of the auditorium.

Later that day after school, I walked the two short blocks to my house very slowly. As I walked I began to think. I thought about a lot of things. I thought about my acting, about my life, and about my future. It is crazy how life can change at the drop of a hat. I really missed parts of the old me. Parts that loved to laugh at silly jokes, to set my friends up on dates, to go to all of the games, and hang out at Sunny Ridge Nursing Home. It was there that I discovered my talent to paint. Things were going so well. I had been dating Patrick since freshman year. I was junior class president, and I was in the middle of painting this beautiful mural for Sunny Ridge. I loved me. I loved my life. I felt good. Finally, I felt whole.

Then one day, I was leaving Sunny Ridge and happened to see Erika and Patrick at the park across the street. I started to walk over, because I thought Patrick would love seeing me. As I got closer, it seemed like they were awfully close. When I was right up on them, I realized they were kissing. I was speechless. I waited for them to explain. Instead I remember Erika making crazy remarks about how I was dressed. I didn't understand why Patrick was laughing and didn't wait to find out. I ran away humiliated. It wasn't until I got home that I realized I was in my painting clothes and I had paint in my hair and on my face. The thing is, I never would have cared about that before, but it occurred to me that I had never let Patrick see me that way. He expected me to be clean and stylish and pretty all of the time, and I kinda fell into that trap. I never let him see me any other way and that totally set up unfair expectations for myself. It hurt when he laughed at me, because there wasn't the make- up or the cute clothes to hide behind. He was actually laughing at me.

It was after I realized that I had been putting on a front

that I decided to drop the "perfect" act and naturally be who I was. Now I am just going to be my regular self and enjoy it!

When I looked up, I was standing in front of my house. I approached the steps and sat down. I looked around and breathed in the cool air. Spring is my favorite season. It's another time of the year where you can actually see the beauty of the earth change into more.

"Hey Minah." A voice called out.

I looked up at the sound and found myself staring into Jeremy's eyes.

"Hi!" I replied, surprised. Jeremy and I rarely talked outside of school and I couldn't remember if he had ever been to my house before. "What's up?"

"What's up? " He repeated smiling. "You were assigned to work with the understudy for Jason right?'

I laughed, suddenly understanding. "I'm sorry. I didn't even know you were in the play," I explained.

Jeremy shrugged his broad shoulders and motioned towards the steps. "Mind if I sit down?"

"Of course not." I scooted over to make room.

"So," Jeremy raised his eye brows.

"So," I repeated. "Look, I'll get straight to the point. I can act. I've been acting for seven years, but I'm still having trouble and ..."

"Hey, slow down," Jeremy responded. "I was just trying to start a conversation. We can work on your lines in a few minutes. If that's okay with you?" He looked at me questioningly.

"Yeah," I answered, feeling surprised again. "I'm sorry. I guess I'm just anxious."

"Well, relax. You know," he pointed out, "we've never actually just sat down and talked before. Alone that is."

"True," I acknowledged. " So, how long have you been acting?"

"Actually, I just started. Well, it will be two years soon. I was just always fascinated by…"He looked at me suddenly embarrassed. "I know you don't want to hear this."

"Jeremy, yeah I do," I encouraged.

"I just like acting, that's all," he finished.

I looked at him curiously, started to say something, then changed my mind. I didn't feel like dragging anything out of anyone. Besides, I didn't really know Jeremy as well as the other guys in our group.

"Well, acting is very easy to enjoy," I smiled. "It's the only time when I can totally disappear and become someone else. I love it."

"Don't you like being yourself also?" he asked.

I shrugged. "I don't know, I guess, sometimes. It just seems like I'm always trying harder than everyone else."

I looked up at the trees. I always ended up with this very empty feeling whenever someone asked me about myself. And suddenly, I wasn't in the mood to think right now, especially about me.

"Why don't we start rehearsing?" I suggested. "Mr. Green will definitely recast me if I don't get these lines."

Jeremy stared at me for a moment, and then nodded. "Okay, well what exactly are you having trouble with?"

Chapter Four

"Which ones? The red or the black?" Mom held up two pair of stiletto heels and waited for my answer.

I turned over on my bed and faced her. "Definitely red. Don't be afraid to make a statement!" I smiled.

"You should take your own advice. What exactly are you wearing anyway?" She frowned.

I looked down at my outfit. Old jean shorts and a grey camp shirt. "Lay off Mom. I'm not going anywhere." I turned away from her.

Mom walked over and sat on the edge of the bed. "Minah, please don't get upset. I don't mean to be on your case. Honey, you've made the first step, you joined the school play, and you even have a new guy friend. But why are you so afraid to show how beautiful you are? And don't even try to say you aren't. You have my genes, you have to be beautiful."

I looked at her and smiled.

"Come with me to the bathroom, I want to show you something." Mom reached out her hand. I took it and followed her to the hall bathroom.

Mom stood me in front of the mirror. "What do you see?"

I stared sadly for a moment, and then said, "Not too much."

"That's because you don't want to see too much," Mom said.

Mom reached behind my head and took my bun out, and let my naturally wavy hair fall to my shoulders. She fluffed it out a bit and ordered me to smile.

"There, now can you see what you're hiding from everyone? You are truly beautiful, inside and out. You don't let anyone see it. The only ones who know who you really are, are Amity and me. You have so much to share, and people deserve to know that. Acting is fine as a hobby, but Minah, life is not a play. Come off stage, honey. Please . . . do it for me, if not for yourself."

I looked at her, and suddenly felt very tired. She was right, I was acting, and I was tired of acting my life out. I couldn't hold back the exhaustion or the tears. I started crying and it seemed like I would never stop. And it seemed like Mom would never stop holding me.

Chapter Five

The first step to regaining your life back lies inside the walls of your neighborhood mall; shopping.

Okay, that's not all true. There are many steps, but by far the most fun is shopping! That's exactly what Mom and I spent the whole entire weekend doing. She canceled all of her appointments, and said she had a family emergency. And in a way she did, her only daughter had just woken up from a year in a coma. Going shopping with my Mom is different than shopping with anyone else. Mom has a few talents, and the greatest one is the ability to shop. Before leaving the house she told me that money was no object, and to throw all of my old clothes out. And because she was paying, I did. Wouldn't you?

"I am so tired. Aren't we almost finished?" I asked.

"You need a spring jacket, and then we'll call it quits," Mom searched through the rack. "Which color?"

"Teal, must you even ask?" I smiled tiredly.

"How about this one?" Mom held up a light jacket made of a dark teal with black stripes.

"I like it. Let's go." I headed toward the exit, while she headed toward the register.

We were finally finished, and as we carried our heavy bags to the car, I finally felt like I was on my way.

"How was your weekend?" Ben asked me during lunch the next day. His eyes held a glimmer of mischief.

"So you noticed?" I fluffed my hair a little and smiled. I had been waiting for someone to notice the difference.

"How could you not notice?" Anthony exclaimed. "You look like an old friend I used to know, but even better."

"Okay, I have an announcement," All eyes at our lunch table turned to Amity. "Minah is out of her funk, she is her old self, no discussion, no questions, and no explanations. Okay?" She looked at everyone.

"Okay," was the unified answer.

"So, Minah, you look very nice," Anthony remarked, and then laughed. "Oh, is it okay to say that?"

"That's a comment I'll take any day," I was wearing one of my new outfits- a long sleek jean skirt and a white top. I laughed, and looked up straight into the eyes of Jeremy.

"Don't forget we have practice after school, Minah," he said.

"Of course not," I smiled.

"Practice for what?" Amity asked curiously.

"Oh. Jeremy is the understudy for Jason, and I have to rehearse my lines with him everyday, that's all, no big deal," I glanced up in time to see a faint look of disappointment on Jeremy's face.

"So, how is the play going anyway?" Anthony asked.

"You ought to know," I scoffed. "You do sets, remember?" Anthony suddenly looked down guiltily.

"Wait!! Don't tell me you haven't been going to rehearsals everyday," Ben shrieked.

"Hey. I thought they would have called me when they needed me," Anthony shrugged his shoulders. "Besides the play isn't for a month. I have plenty of time."

"Well I hope you know how to design a complete carnival scene," I stated. "Because that's one of the six sets that they'll need."

"If they want a carnival scene, then they'll have one," Anthony assured us. He looked around at all of the doubtful expressions. "Hey! Don't worry! I'll take care of it."

"Minah, I was wondering if we could practice a little earlier today?" Jeremy asked quietly.

I took a sip of water. "Sure. Why earlier?"

"I promised Amy Banks that I would help her with her lines," He looked at me guiltily.

"Well, that's fine," I said nonchalantly. For some reason I had a strange feeling in my stomach. It felt slightly like jealousy. But why would I be jealous? I dismissed the thought and turned to talk to Amity.

Chapter Six

For some reason, I keep thinking about Jeremy and Amy Banks. That's absurd, because I don't have any sort of claim on Jeremy, and I don't know anything about Amy Banks. But nonetheless, these strange ideas keep popping into my head. Like, "I wonder what they're doing right now, and I wonder if he laughs as much with her as he does with me?"

I mean, who am I to have these thoughts?

"Minah! Telephone!" Mom yelled.

I jerked out of my thoughts quickly. I hadn't even heard the phone. I reached across my bed to the nightstand and picked up the phone. "I have it." I said.

"Hi, Minah," It was Jeremy.

"Oh, hi Jeremy. What's up?" I asked casually.

"Do you have some time to talk?" he asked.

"Sure," I said getting excited. "Do you want to come over?"

"Okay. I'll be there in fifteen minutes," Jeremy replied.

"Fine. I'll be waiting," I hung up the phone with a smile on my face. There could only be one reason that Jeremy would want to talk to me, and I knew what it was. He wanted to tell me that he liked me. That would be perfect, because then I could tell him that I liked him too.

I rushed around, trying to straighten up the house and myself at the same time. It wasn't easy. By the time the doorbell rang, I was out of breath. "Mom, can you get the door please?" I begged.

Mom responded with a sigh and a smile. "Sure, but isn't it just Jeremy?"

A second later she called, "Minah you have a visitor." There was a smile in her voice.

I walked downstairs quickly, smoothing my hair as I did. "Hi Jeremy," I said, as I came to a stop next to Mom. I was suddenly a bit nervous.

"Hey Minah," He answered.

"Jeremy, I want you to meet my mother Lavendar. Mom meet Jeremy, he just moved to San Jose."

"Nice to meet you Ms..."

"You can call me Lavendar, all of Minah's friends do," Mom smiled.

"So do you want to talk in my room?" I asked Jeremy.

He looked over at me and shrugged. "That's fine."

We said good-bye to Mom, and walked up the stairs towards my room. "Sorry if it's kinda junky, we went shopping over the weekend." I apologized as I opened the door.

Jeremy's eye lit up as he stepped inside, "This is really nice."

"Sit down," I invited, pointing towards the couch.

Jeremy sat down, and I followed suit. "So," I began. "What do you want to talk about?" I was smiling inside; I couldn't wait to hear this. I silently counted to 5 to calm myself down.

"I met a really nice girl…"

"What!" I interrupted.

"…and I need some advice." Jeremy started. "Out of our group, you're the girl that I feel most comfortable talking to, and I need some advice."

'Um, okay. I'll try," I said, getting an uneasy feeling.

"Well, it's Amy," Jeremy began.

My stomach dropped as I realized what Jeremy was about to say. I swear I didn't want to hear it. I couldn't bear it.

I tried to smile, but nodded my head instead.

"Well, I just met her, but she seems really nice, and I think she likes me too. I just don't know how to ask her out," He looked at me. "I thought maybe you could help me think of a way. I mean we've gotten kinda close, and I wanted to hear a girl's opinion."

"Mine?!" I squeaked. "Do you know how long it's been since I went out on a date?"

Jeremy shook his head.

"At least a year. I'm the wrong person to ask. Haven't Ben and Anthony told you my story?"

"What story? Besides I don't see how someone as beautiful as you could not have dates all of the time," Jeremy answered.

I shifted his focus. "Well, Amy's beautiful too. Isn't she?" I remarked sarcastically.

Jeremy looked at me funny, and prepared to respond.

"Never mind," I said shaking my head, suddenly feeling very selfish and mean. After all, Jeremy was my friend. "The easiest way to ask a girl out is to just ask her."

"That's easier said than done," Jeremy said softly. He touched my shoulder. "Look, I'm not the most outspoken person in case you haven't noticed."

"Well, I haven't noticed," I said incredulously, moving aside. "You've never had a problem talking to me or Amity."

"That's because you guys are my friends," He stated simply,

"Right," I said. I took a deep breath. The last thing I wanted to do was give him advice on how to ask someone else out.

"Look, I don't know what to say. Ask her or don't ask her. It's up to you."

I threw my hands up.

Jeremy looked at me. "Look, I thought I could ask you for a favor, but I guess I was wrong." He stood up and walked to the door.

"Wait!" I cried out. "Jeremy, I'm sorry. You just caught me on a bad day. I don't know what to say."

"Just forget it." He said shortly.

"We're still practicing tomorrow, right?" I asked hopefully.

Jeremy stared at me for a few seconds, "Sure. That's what we agreed to. I'll see you later." He prepared to open the door.

I jumped up. "Let me walk you to the front door."

"That's okay," he responded. "I know the way out."

Slowly, I sat back down as the door closed behind him.

Chapter Seven

$\mathcal{I}$ decided to call Amity. It was time that I let my best friend in on my life. I picked up the phone, punched in the numbers, and waited to hear her voice.

"Hello," It wasn't Amity; it was her sister.

"Hi Jeannie. Is Amity home?" I asked.

"Sure. Hold on Minah." I heard the phone drop, Jeannie's yell, and then the footsteps as Amity walked to the phone.

"Hey, Minah. Long time, no hear," Amity said, laughing. Amity has a tendency to forget that she isn't actually the funniest person in the world, but I had to laugh too, because that's what you do most with Amity.

"What are you doing?" I asked.

"Nothing. The TV was on, but for some reason I have no desire to watch," Amity's voice suddenly dropped.

Oh lord, here we go, I thought.

I knew she was waiting for me to ask what was wrong.

"What?" I asked. "Is it Justin?"

"Yeah," Amity sighed. "We broke up."

Now right here is where you would expect me to either be happy or sad for my friend. But to be honest I couldn't really feel anything. Justin was a guy I never even met. Amity met him at summer camp, so none of us were able to meet him. He was like a ghost. But still, I felt bad for her because I knew that she really liked him. Personally, I thought she could do better. With a blunt hairstyle, pretty brown eyes, cute nose, and I guess a nice figure, Amity had never lost the attention of guys. She was always turning down dates, because of her loyalty to Justin. But like Jeremy, she seemed not to be aware of her looks. I really liked that. With a mother that's in the fashion business, you have a tendency to meet a lot of conceited people. I don't see how Mom can stand to be around them. She is far from conceited, but she does describe herself as confident. It's something she believes everyone should be.

"I'm sorry Amity," I replied. "Are you alright?"

"Yeah. It was kinda getting hard to keep the long distance thing going," Amity's voice went up again. "But forget about that. Why'd you call?

I climbed on my bed, rolled over onto my stomach, put my feet in the air, and prepared to talk. "It's going to surprise you." I started.

"Let me guess," Amity said. "Docs this have to do with a guy that has the following characteristics: dark brown eyes, black hair, very nice body..."

I could just see her using her fingers to mark off these traits. To me that just seemed funny, and the fact that my secret wasn't a secret was even funnier.

"Okay, Miss Know it All," I said laughing.

"Well Minah, I'm your best friend. I would have to be blind not to notice if you had a crush on someone. Besides,

I saw your expression at lunch when he mentioned Amy. Now, what happened?"

Quickly, I filled Amity in on the events of the afternoon. I examined my nails as I waited for her answer.

"Okay, first of all, why in the world didn't you call me earlier?" she accused. "And second, did you ever think that the reason he got so upset was because maybe he likes you too?"

I jumped off the bed. "Hey. Do you really think so? Then why would he ask me for help with Amy?"

Amity was silent for a second considering her own suggestion.

"Because that's how he is. Yeah," She said finally. "I do think so. I've seen the way he looks at you. Maybe he was testing you to see what you'd say. Wait, hang on a second."

She clicked over to her other line.

A few seconds later she came back on the line. "Minah, that's Daniel Woods. He wants to ask me out. Word got out fast!" Amity's voice was close to shrill.

"Well for goodness sake!" I screamed happily. "Get off the phone with me, and go get that date. You're single now."

"Alright! See ya later," Amity replied excitedly. "Oh yeah, Minah," she called out. "Think about what I said."

And for the whole night, that's exactly what I did.

Chapter Eight

"Jeremy!" I was half walking, half running to catch up to him. "Wait up!"

He turned around and I paused as his brown eyes bore into mine.

I walked towards him and tried to keep my hands from shaking. As I got close, I noticed his eyes looked troubled; I hoped he wasn't still mad at me.

"What's up?" He asked solemnly. He was not his usual self.

"Are you still mad at me?" I asked desperately. "I'm sorry, it's just that ..."

"Oh, no!" Jeremy looked surprised. "I really wasn't thinking about it. Actually I am upset, but it's not with you...anymore," he said pointedly. "Mr. Green just told me that I have to take over for Jason. I guess 'the jock' is too busy to act after all."

"Well, that's good news," I looked at him happily. I was glad he wasn't mad at me. Then I noticed a frown on his face. "Wait, isn't it?"

"Well, yeah I guess so. But I have never really acted in front of a large audience," Jeremy looked away.

"What?!" I exclaimed. "But you told me that you had been acting for two years."

"Well, I went to drama camp for two summers," Jeremy looked ashamed. "I didn't want you to make fun of me, or think that I didn't know what I was talking about. I mean, I was sent to help you, remember?"

I sighed and put my hand on Jeremy's shoulder. "Jeremy, that's not what matters. You are a great actor. You got me saying my lines right. So now I'll help you. Deal?"

Those gorgeous eyes looked into mine and I heard him say, "Deal." But all of a sudden, I just wanted to kiss him. I stepped back and I know my face was filled with confusion.

Jeremy seemed a little surprised but he just smiled and shrugged his shoulders. "So when can we get started?" he asked.

"Pretty soon," I wanted to focus, I swear I did. But all I saw was his Polo shirt, his khaki pants, and his loafers. Preppy is definitely attractive. Oh yeah, it is.

I mentally shook myself and forced my mind to concentrate.

"That's a nice outfit," Jeremy commented, looking me over.

Great! Like complimenting me was going to solve my problem, I don't think so. I looked down; I had worn a jean jacket, small white shirt with matching jeans and white mules. "Thanks."

We started walking out the school door and decided that we would walk to Jeremy's to start the coaching.

It was a beautiful day, just like most days in March, in

San Jose at least. I really loved this city. I was born and raised here, and would miss it when I went to college.

"So, do you like San Jose?" I asked Jeremy. Suddenly I was more curious about him.

He shifted his backpack on his back and smiled. "Yeah, I do. It's a great city. I've met some cool people. Especially you guys," His smile broadened. "I think Anthony and Ben are some of the best friends I've ever met. Amity is really sweet and down to earth....," he paused glancing at me. "You're really cool too, easy to talk to, fun to hang out with. And you are one of the prettiest girls I've ever met."

I looked at him surprised. "Even prettier than Amy Banks?" There was teasing in my voice.

"Amy who?" he asked innocently.

It was then that I understood Amy was no longer a factor. That was definitely a good thing. We had stopped walking and were now in front of his house.

"So, you ready to start?" he asked me, his beautiful smile at its best.

"Sure," I agreed as we walked inside.

"Hello Jeremy," Jeremy's mom said.

"Hey Mom. Guess who got the lead in the school play?" Jeremy asked smiling.

"Let me guess," Mrs. Smith said playfully. "The best understudy in the world?"

"Yeah," Jeremy went to hug his mom.

"Congratulations!" Mrs. Smith noticed me standing there. "Oh, hello Minah."

She gave Jeremy another quick hug and leaned over to hug me.

"Hi, Mrs. Smith. How are you?" I responded warmly.

"Fine," Jeremy's mom is pretty in that casual, southern way. Today she had on jeans, a flannel shirt, and her hair was pulled back into a pony tail. "Great outfit." she remarked. "I swear, I still haven't gotten used to these California styles."

"Thanks," I said proudly to her first remark. "California has to grow on you. What are you working on now?" Jeremy's mother was an artist. Our group had met her at an art exhibit at our school.

"Well, actually," Mrs. Smith looked sheepish. "I'm working on the kitchen and bedrooms," she started laughing. "I'm painting the house. Jeremy's Dad's doing the outside, and I'm doing the inside, with the Jeremy and Jacob's help, of course!"

Jacob was Jeremy's older brother; he went to school at U.C. Berkeley and only came home on the weekends and holidays.

"Well if you need any help, I'll leave my number so you can call," I volunteered. "I love painting. I painted my own room actually, you should see it."

Jeremy looked surprised. "You did that? It looked professional."

"Thanks Jeremy, I worked hard on it," I looked at him expectantly. "So I guess we better start, huh?"

"Yeah," Jeremy faced his mother. "Mom we're going to go over some lines in my room."

"Okay. Minah want to stay for dinner? I'm making chicken pot pies from scratch!" she said, her eyes shining.

"That sounds good. I'll call my mom," I answered.

Quickly, I got the okay from my mom and went upstairs to Jeremy's room. His room was the complete opposite of mine. Not as flashy. Not as two toned. But it was still nice. He had a full size bed covered by a deep royal blue comforter. He had a rocking chair in one corner, a book case in another, and a desk adjacent to the bed. It was more dignified compared to my drastic artistic atmospheric bedroom.

"I like this room, plus it's neat," I pointed out. "I never knew guys knew how to clean their rooms." I sat down in the rocking chair.

"Not all guys are messy," Jeremy argued, smiling.

"Anyway, enough talk. Let's get to work."

For a full three hours, Jeremy and I studied his lines and mine as well. We worked on his voice inflection and projection. In all honesty, Jeremy was a terrific actor, and I had confidence that he would do well.

When I felt we had done enough, I threw the script on the bed and stood up to stretch.

"Acting can be exhausting," Jeremy remarked as he stretched too.

"Yeah, it can be," I said thoughtfully.

Jeremy was sitting on the bed, and I went over and sat next to him.

"So what did you think?" I asked, looking at him.

He ran his hand over his face. "I think we work well together."

"So do I." My voice was soft. Some force pushed me forward and our faces came together. Slowly we came closer. Suddenly there was a knock on the door, and we sprang apart.

"Jeremy, Minah, dinner!" Mrs. Smith called.

I looked back at Jeremy. We smiled weakly at each other, then stood up and walked out the door.

"Dinner was great Mrs. Smith," I praised.

"Well, you'll have to come back when I cook," Mr. Smith remarked. "Then you'll see some real cooking."

Mrs. Smith's eyebrows went up.

"Just kidding, sweetheart." Mr. Smith gave her a kiss on the cheek and she beamed.

"Minah do you want a ride home?" Jeremy asked.

"Sure," I agreed, standing up. I put my dishes in the sink, reminded Mrs. Smith to call me if she needed help, said good-bye, and then followed Jeremy outside.

Jeremy opened the car door for me, then went on the driver's side and got in.

"Nice car," I commented, unconsciously fluffing

my hair. It felt so good to let my hair down -no pun intended- but I had gotten so tired of that bun.

"Thank you," Jeremy replied. He put his hands firmly on the steering wheel and backed out of the driveway. "It was a gift for my sixteenth birthday."

I knew Jeremy was now seventeen, and his car still looked brand new. I took that as a good sign. He took care of his things . . . and hopefully his girlfriends as well.

"When's your birthday?" I asked curiously.

"October 23," he said. "When's yours?"

"April 12." I looked at him. He was a very confident driver and seemed to know the streets well. Then again, I only lived five blocks from him. I also had my license, but, like Jeremy, I didn't feel it was necessary to drive to school; we lived so close.

"Well, here we are," Jeremy announced.

Unbeknownst to me, we had already pulled up in front of my house. The whole ride had taken less than five minutes. I really didn't want to leave, and I tried to think of a way to stall. Suddenly the answer came to me. Now was the perfect time to tell Jeremy how I felt. And I was already pretty sure that he felt the same way; now we could get it out in the open.

"Jeremy, I need to talk to you," I took a deep breath. "It's really important that you let me say everything before you speak."

"Okay." Jeremy looked serious. He licked his lips and waited.

"This is very awkward for me," I sighed. "I have never done this before."

"Minah, just take a deep breath, and tell me whatever you need to tell me," Jeremy suggested softly.

I took that deep breath and looked at him squarely in the face. "I have feelings for you."

Jeremy started to nod, but I shook my head. "More than friendship feelings," I argued. "I didn't want to say anything, and when you brought up Amy Banks, I knew I couldn't," I paused. "But I changed my mind. I want you to know."

All of a sudden I couldn't stop smiling. "Jeremy, you are different from any guy I've ever known and during the time we've been working together, I feel that we've gotten to know each other," I looked at him shyly. "I care about you Jeremy, and I need you to know that."

"Minah, I'm flattered," Jeremy shook his head. "But..."

I caught the "but", and I didn't like the sound of it. I decided to save face. "You know what? Maybe I just got the wrong idea. My mom's waiting for me, so, um, never mind okay? I'll see you tomorrow," I paused, my hand pushing the door open. "Wait, tomorrow's Saturday, so I guess I'll see you Monday." I was babbling and I couldn't stop.

"But Minah, listen to me," Jeremy began. He reached out to stop me.

"No," I turned to face him. "Let's just forget it," I said simply. I got out of the car. "It was a mistake. Sorry." I slammed the car door shut, and ran into the house.

I didn't even go to Mom's room to say hi. How could I think he actually liked me? I let my imagination, not to mention Amity's, get away with me. I went directly to my room, threw myself across the bed, and cried until there were no tears left.

Chapter Nine

I woke up with the sun shining on my face, and it was a deep contrast to what I was feeling inside. I felt anything but cheery. I opened my eyes. I looked down and saw that the covers had been pulled up on me, but I was still in my clothes from yesterday. That wasn't good. I sat up, stretched, and got out of bed. I decided to take a shower and just bum around the house for the day.

After my shower I threw on a Mickey Mouse t-shirt, some red sweat shorts and pulled my hair high on my head in a pom-pom ponytail. I ran down to the kitchen and after looking through the cabinets decided on corn flakes with sliced bananas. On the weekends, I had to get my own breakfast, because Mom worked early, but on the weekdays she always made great breakfasts, and then went to work.

I sat down at the table, and looked around the sunny, yellow kitchen. I knew it was almost noon, and I felt like I should be doing something. But I really didn't feel like it. I continued eating. Then put my dishes in the sink, took down some Oreos from the pantry and went into the family room to watch T.V. I knew Amity wouldn't come over because today was her date with Daniel Woods.

I stretched out on the burgundy couch, put a pillow behind my head and flipped on the TV. Just then the doorbell rang.

"Who could that be?" I mumbled as I got up.

I walked to the door and peeked out the hole. It was Jeremy.

"Great," I grumbled. I looked back through the peephole. He looked very nice. He had on jean shorts and a Sonics t-shirt. I debated whether or not to let him in and decided to do it.

"Hi Jeremy," I said, looking over his head.

"Can I come in?" he asked searching for my eyes. "I need to talk to you."

There was no point in postponing the inevitable. "Sure." I widened the door and directed him to the family room.

We both sat on the couch, and I waited for him to speak.

"Minah, I really like you," Jeremy was speaking quickly.

I started to shake my head, partly to clear my ears. I know I hadn't heard right. "But last night you said BUT..."

"I was going to say, 'But I didn't think you were interested in me'. But you didn't let me finish," Jeremy smiled ruefully.

"No, I didn't," I nodded. "I didn't want to hear anything bad. How embarrassing. I just didn't want to hear you reject me."

Jeremy thought about that. "That's understandable. But if you run away, you might miss out on the good stuff too."

"Yeah, you're right," I smiled shyly looking at him.

"I'm sorry about last night."

"Don't apologize. I'm not sorry," Jeremy's voice dropped.

Our heads came together and this time no one interrupted us. Our lips met in a soft kiss and my whole face heated up. I slowly pulled away.

"That was nice," I smiled.

Jeremy touched my neck and slowly pulled me back towards him. This time the kiss lasted longer, we pulled away at the same time and looked at each other.

"Minah, I really like you a lot," Jeremy sighed. "Let's go out tonight."

I looked at him surprised. That wasn't what I was expecting him to say, but I felt relief that he did. "I like that idea," I agreed.

We agreed to go to dinner and a movie, and a few minutes later Jeremy had to leave to run errands for his mom. I stayed at the front door watching him, and I promise you, I couldn't stop smiling. Reluctantly I watched his car drive away, and then I closed the door and ran up to my room to choose an outfit.

I opened the closet and just stared. "Well, at least I know I'll have something to wear," I muttered. The closet was packed with all of the new clothes from my shopping spree. Did I want to look casual, dressy, sexy, subtle?

"Minah, are you home?" It was Mom.

I knew she would be so happy when she heard the news. I ran downstairs and jumped right into her arms.

"Well hello to you too," she said with a smile. I stepped back and looked at her outfit which was now wrinkled thanks to me. A lime green shorts suit with lime sandals. It was cute.

"Sorry," I apologized.

Mom looked unconcerned. "You know I don't care.

What's up?"

I followed her into the kitchen and watched as she poured herself some cranberry juice. "Guess who asked me out?" I said mysteriously.

Mom took a minute to pretend like she was thinking. Then shrugged her shoulders and smiled. "Jeremy," she answered matter of factly.

"How did you know?" I asked, surprised. Jeremy and I had always seemed just like friends to me.

"Minah, a mother knows," she said wisely.

I just smiled.

"So," she said importantly, "what are you going to wear?"

We decided on a brown corduroy miniskirt with a tight tan t-shirt. I slipped a brown pair of sandals on my feet, and turned to the mirror to do my hair. I couldn't decide whether to wear it up or down; I decided to do both. I pulled my bangs to the side and pulled some of my hair up in a butterfly clip, and let the back hang to my shoulders.

"I like this look," I complimented myself. I put on some dusty brown eye shadow, some Rum Raisin lipstick, sprayed on a delicate perfume, and I was ready.

As I went to my room to grab my purse, I heard the doorbell. "I have it," Mom called up.

I walked down in time to hear Mom commenting on Jeremy's outfit. I had to agree that he looked very nice. Jeremy had on black jeans with a white, short sleeve mock turtleneck, and black boots. Very stylish.

When Jeremy saw me, his eyes lit up. "Hey Minah, you look nice."

"Thank you," I replied, my eyes bright.

"Well, I guess you two better get going," Mom prodded.

"Nice seeing you again Ms...Lavendar," Jeremy caught himself.

"Bye, you guys." Mom whisked us out the door. She

had an Eric Jerome Dickey book in one hand. She had been waiting forever to finish that book.

"Do you think she wanted to get rid of us?" Jeremy asked, amused.

"Maybe. But I don't mind," I answered.

I walked to his car and he opened the door for me. I stepped inside and when I was settled, he closed the door.

I waited for him to get in. "You look nice, Jeremy," I said.

"So do you," He leaned over and kissed my cheek.

"So where are we going?" I asked curiously.

"Well there's this great place downtown that my mother told me about," Jeremy began as we pulled off. "It's on San Pedro, and it serves great Italian food."

"Oh you mean The Spaghetti Factory!" I exclaimed. "That's my favorite restaurant. The spumoni is delicious."

"Good. Then we'll enjoy it," Jeremy replied happily.

It was after we had finished our dinner, that I took time to just admire Jeremy. I started laughing.

Jeremy look at me, amused. "What?"

I giggled and said. "I was just wondering what Ben and Anthony are going to say when they find out about us."

"You guys are really close, huh?" Jeremy said.

"Oh," I said. "We've all been tight since we were kids. We've been through so much together. They're like my brothers. I'm an only child so it's cool to have a family like that."

"And Amity's your sister?" He questioned.

"Yeah my sister and my best friend," I turned solemn. "The whole gang stood by me during my metamorphosis."

"What exactly happened?" Jeremy asked curiously. "When I met you, all I knew was that old you, and now you're a new you, but actually it's the old you."

I looked at him shocked, "If I didn't know what you were talking about, I would be totally confused. Right now

I'm only a little confused."

"But you know what I mean," Jeremy said hurriedly.

"Yeah. I do," I grasped for an explanation. "Let's just say when me and my ex- boyfriend broke up, I thought it was because I was lacking, so I blamed myself." I looked around. "I didn't think I was ready for a boyfriend, so I decided to get away from that whole scene."

I caught him shaking his head. "I know," I agreed. "It's crazy, no one understood, least of all me. But I got my grades up, I focused on me more, and I stayed on track."

"And what made you go back to your old self?" Jeremy questioned, interested.

"Oh, I'll never be my old self," I disagreed. "I was younger then, I've matured now. So I've already changed." I sighed. "I just got tired of pretending to be happy. I knew what it took to be really happy, so I got help from my mom and friends," I stopped and smiled. "And Ta Da!"

"I like this you, Minah," Jeremy commented. "But then again I liked you the other way also," He paused and studied my face. "Even if you were trying to stop guys from noticing you, it didn't work."

I looked at him, surprised. "What do you mean?"

"There were quite a few guys that had crushes on you, and probably still do," Jeremy answered. "They always told me because they knew we were friends. You can't hide true beauty."

I smiled shyly. "I guess we should get going. The movie starts at 9:00."

Jeremy stood up and came around the table and pulled my chair out for me.

"I don't think I've ever known a guy that has such good manners," I remarked.

"I was raised to always treat women the way I would want my mother treated," Jeremy smiled. "And I would want her to be treated like a queen."

I felt my eyes grow moist. "That's so sweet."

"It's true," Jeremy threw his hands up. "So you're ready?"

"Yeah, I am." We walked to the car and headed towards the movies.

Instead of seeing a recent movie, we had decided to see a restoration of <u>An Affair to Remember</u>. It was one of my favorite romance movies, and Jeremy had never seen it. I loved that he wasn't afraid to see a romantic movie with me.

We held hands during the whole movie, and when I cried he gave me a hug. I felt like I was in heaven.

"I had a wonderful time tonight," We were at my front door and Jeremy was preparing to say good-bye.

"Maybe," I teased. "But probably not as much as me." I put my arms around him and pulled him close. "So when will I see you next?"

Jeremy leaned down and kissed my cheek. "Soon. Goodnight."

"Goodnight." I opened the door and stepped inside.

Chapter Ten

"Okay, so basically you're dating?" Amity was sprawled across my love seat, a bag of dried apricots in her hand. Her hair was hanging in her face, and it covered one eye. She looked ridiculous and I had to laugh.

"I don't know," I answered. I was lying on my bed eating an apple. "I mean what if I think we're dating, but we're not?"

"Minah, to me it sounds like a couple sort of thing," she reasoned. "I mean, honestly, wouldn't you call it that if it was some other couple?"

I sat up and thought for a second. "Yeah. I guess so," I sighed. "I really like him a lot. He's so sweet, and kind, and cute." I giggled.

"Yeah, yeah. I know." Amity rolled her eyes.

"So what's up for today?" We had already gone to church and we had a whole Sunday free.

"Don't know. We could jog around Lake Cunningham," She suggested. "We did say we would do that on a free day."

"Well, I have nothing else to do, and I refuse to sit around just thinking about Jeremy." I began tying my sneakers.

"Then let's go now. I'm bored," Amity pleaded.

"Thanks a lot," I remarked wryly.

"Not because of you," She assured me.

"Never mind, let's just go," I said bouncing up.

Awhile later we began our jog. It was a beautiful day. Nice and sunny, but enough wind to cool down any heat the sun may force on us. We started off slow and gradually built up a pace. Amity is a stronger runner than me, so I usually work off her.

It was while we were coming to a bend that I lost my balance. Out of nowhere it seemed a rock appeared, and although I am not usually clumsy, I fell right over it, and because Amity was in front of me, she went down too. (Maybe because I fell into her.)

"What the heck?" Amity did not look pleased, and when she tried to stand up I saw why; she had twisted her ankle.

I tried to help her, but when I began to stand, I fell right back down. It looked like I had twisted my ankle too. The irony was too much. Amity's face changed from a frown to a grin, and we both burst out laughing. And that's how we looked when Ben, Anthony, and Jeremy walked up to us.

Ben spoke first. "I don't even want to ask what happened." He shook his head and paused.

When we didn't say anything, he said, "OK, I changed my mind, what happened?"

As I explained, the guys hauled us up off the ground.

They couldn't help but laugh too. Amity and I looked amused while Anthony, Ben and Jeremy leaned on each other and let out huge guffaws.

"So, how did you guys get here?" Anthony asked smirking, as they started to calm down.

"I drove, luckily," I answered. The car was about a quarter of a mile away, but we made it. I took awhile, hurt a lot, and at times they had to carry us, but we made it.

During the whole thing, I noticed that Jeremy hadn't said anything. Anthony and Ben decided to get me in the car first since I was driving. Luckily, I had hurt my left foot so I could still use my right foot to drive. I mean, if I was careful, I thought, we may make it home in one piece. But before they could act on this plan, Jeremy cut in.

"I'm driving you home. Ben, take my car home please." Jeremy came around to the side to help Amity and myself in. "We don't want to take any more risks. You just take care of that foot." He looked at me strangely but smiled.

"Is anything wrong?" I asked, concerned, as Jeremy started driving.

"No." A quick answer. He glanced in the rearview mirror and switched lanes.

"Jeremy, I can tell that something is bothering you." I tried to take my mind off of the pain. And I wanted to know why he was acting like a stranger!

"You don't need to make everything so public!" He glanced at me then towards the back seat where Amity was sitting. Of course Amity was listening to everything.

"Jeremy, I don't think any one really cares. I was just concerned," I said simply. "Besides, Amity knows about us."

Amity spoke up softly. "Pretend like I'm not here. Really, I wish I wasn't."

"Minah, let's not do this right now."

"Do what!?" I was getting upset. "I only asked you what was wrong."

"Nothing." We pulled into my driveway. Jeremy looked at me. "You need to get your ankle looked at. You guys take care. I'll call you later."

"Yeah, do that, after your attitude changes." I allowed him to help us to the door and watched as he walked off.

"So what do you think that was all about?!" Amity was spread out on one couch, and I was on the other.

We had just returned from the emergency room. Amity was forced to stay with us for a few days because her mom was out of town. Usually she stayed home alone, but because of her ankle, she couldn't be by herself. Mom loved Amity, and asked her to stay with us. And I was glad, because it would be less boring with company. Come to find out, we actually had sprained ankles. It was a complete coincidence that we both had the same injury.

Mom had settled us in the family room where the TV was. She brought us some drinks, magazines and books to take our minds off the pain.

I rolled over, careful to mind the bandage on my ankle and looked at her. "I don't know. It was like he was another person today."

"You know what I think?" Amity propped up on one elbow.

I rolled my eyes, "What?"

"He's scared to let you get too close, because he thinks he might hurt you." She looked at me sensibly. "You know, after all of the drama you've been through. It probably scares him a little."

"But that's silly. I've really changed, and that had nothing to do with him, that was about me." I was trying to convince Amity.

"I know that, Ben and Anthony know that, your mom knows it. But, Jeremy's going off the stories that he's heard. He did only come here in December, it's only March now. He hasn't really known any of us for very long. He's closer to the guys than us." Amity thought for a second. "Guys talk and the fellas probably told him about your phase, but never in a bad way. Face it that would still be a little risky for a guy that really likes you. He would blame himself. What if you have a relapse?"

"But I'm not going to!" I said. The more I thought about it, the more exasperating it got. "Maybe it's not worth it!" I yelled. It's crazy thinking about how low I let my self esteem get, and over a guy! Now when I'm trying to build it back up, I have more drama, and yeah, over a guy!

"Yes it is worth it. I know you are trying, but maybe he doesn't." Amity threw her hands in the air. "But then again, I'm a girl, and he's a guy, therefore he's ..."

"SLOWER," we said together.

That was our private joke. Whenever a guy didn't respond the way we thought he should, we blamed it on him being slower than us. It may not be true, but it made us feel better.

"Anyway, he sounded angry," I brought up.

"So what!!" Amity looked at me. "You've been talking about this for the last two hours. I'm in pain. I'm medicated, and I'm tired. I'm going to take a nap."

I looked at her, shocked.

"Minah, I 'm sorry," Her voice softened. "But seriously, my foot hurts and I'm getting crabby. Just let me rest for awhile and we'll talk later. Plus we'll have all of tomorrow. Neither one of us can go to school." she smiled.

I smiled, understanding completely and suddenly aware of the pain in my own foot. "A nap does sound good."

So we both settled in on our respective couches and fell asleep.

Chapter Eleven

*I*t was a few days later that I finally heard from Jeremy.

Because of my sprained ankle, I couldn't go to school, and Jeremy had never called. Amity's mom started home as soon as she heard about the accident and Amity was now back to the comforts of her own house. When the phone rang in the afternoon, I knew it was him.

"Hello," I answered.

"Hi, Minah. It's Jeremy. I wanted to know if I could come over." His voice was low and serious.

"Well Jeremy, I don't know. Are you sure your friends wouldn't mind?" My voice was sarcastic.

He sighed. "So, can I come?"

"I've been stuck in my house for three days and this is the first I've heard from you."

"Minah, please, can I come over?" He pleaded.

"Yeah. Come over." And I hung up.

Twenty minutes later there was a knock on my bedroom door.

"Come in." I was reading a book.

"Hi." Jeremy looked shy and a little nervous. I put down the book and just looked at him.

"May I sit down?" He asked politely. I nodded towards the love seat.

"Okay Jeremy, I let you come over, even though you've obviously been ignoring me. What's up?"

"I deserve that." Jeremy looked at me. "You look nice Minah."

I was wearing pajama pants and a purple tank top. "Jeremy, what do you want?"

"This isn't easy for me," Jeremy started.

"This isn't easy for **you**?" I repeated astonished. "Excuse me, but weren't you the one that went through some kind of emotional whirlwind?" I stood up and limped towards him. My voice was calm, but very full of venom. "I thought you liked me, you said you liked me, then like that," I snapped my fingers "You acted like you didn't even know me. My ego can't take these kinds of games right now. "

"I know, I'm sorry." Jeremy was holding his head in his hands. "I did like you, I still do like you."

"Just tell me," I said quietly, sitting back down. "Just explain...NOW."

"Minah." Jeremy got up from the couch and walked to the opposite side of the room. I turned around to watch him. "I had a lot of fun last weekend. I really did. I've never known anyone like you."

"Then what went wrong?" I was confused.

Jeremy walked over to me slowly. He put his hands on my hair and looked into my eyes. "I got scared. What I felt for you was the strongest sensation I have ever felt. I thought it would go away." He leaned down and kissed the tip of my nose. "But it only got stronger. Minah, I thought maybe I was crazy to feel like that so soon. Is that strange?"

"No." My eyes shone bright. "Because I feel the exact same way. That's why it hurt so much."

"I'm stupid." Jeremy drew me into a hug. "Forgive me? It won't happen again, I promise."

"You're forgiven." I looked up and slowly kissed him.

Chapter Twelve

*I*t was the following Monday when Amity and I felt well enough to go back to school. Though we were both on crutches, we were able to move around easily. Mr. Green allowed me to sit during rehearsals for the time being. I was supposed to start going back to Sunny Ridge to do art projects, but I would have to wait a few more weeks for that.

"So the clumsies are back." Ben dropped his tray on the lunch table and sat down.

"How are you two feeling?" Anthony's face looked sincere, but there was laughter in his eyes.

"Honestly, you guys are so sensitive," I said dryly.

"Oh come on Minah. We've called you and Amity everyday since the accident. I think Lavendar and Susan are sick of hearing our voices.

Ben took a bite out of his hamburger.

"Maybe. But I'm glad you guys called. Thanks," I responded smiling.

"Where's Jeremy?" Amity asked me as she started on her salad.

"Here I am." Jeremy came up behind me, then leaned over and kissed me on the cheek.

"Ooh," everyone crooned.

"Oh, shut up." I was laughing.

"You guys know what's coming up don't you?" Jeremy took a bite of pickle.

"The senior ball, Grad Nite, and the senior trip," Amity listed, smiling. "And I can't wait."

"Well, we're doing everything together, right?" Anthony looked at all of us.

"Anthony, sweetheart," I put my hand on top of his. "Is there any other way? Of course we'll be together."

"So, where are all of the events?" Jeremy asked.

"Well, I know Grad Nite takes place in LA, Senior Ball in the Fairmont, and Senior trip in Puerto Vallarta," I supplied.

"Does everyone have the funds?" Ben asked. "You know the sum will come out to at least $500."

"Well, I should have that by the end of April," Amity announced, "My babysitting jobs are mounting up."

"Yeah, I'll have it," I had been saving up for a year. "It's going to be hot." Ben exclaimed.

"When we're together, it always is." I smiled.

Chapter Thirteen

"So you're coming with me to pick out a dress, right?" I was talking on the phone to Amity and painting my toenails at the same time. The bandage had come off that afternoon and I was celebrating.

"Sure Minah. But it'll have to be tomorrow. You know every Saturday I baby-sit for the McLaughlins."

"I don't know why you even bother," I sighed. "I mean you don't even have the patience to be a baby-sitter."

"Well Mr. and Mrs. McLaughlin think I do," she huffed. "Besides, if I want to do all the senior stuff, I have to raise all of the money. You know that."

"Yeah, you're right," I perked up my voice. "Besides you only have a few jobs left until you have all of the money. Gives you *plenty* of time to meet the deadline."

"Speaking of time," Amity said. "Why are you in such a hurry to buy your prom dress? We still have more than a month."

"I know," I agreed. "But Mom gave me a tip on this new designer that released a trial line of formal wear. It's only a quarter of what the real price would be, but they need to test it out on the mere mortals first. The line closes in two weeks. What if it takes me that long to find the right dress?"

"Okay, drama queen," Amity said laughing. "We'll go tomorrow. Hey, maybe I'll even find something."

"Of course you will. That's the spirit. Well I better get off the phone. I need to finish my book report for Monday." I swung my legs off of the bed.

"Yeah, and I need to get to my job. I'll talk to you later." Amity hung up.

I sat on the bed for a few more minutes and reluctantly thought about the book report. I don't mind reading; I even like it, but I hate writing about what I read. But luckily I'm good at it. That's why I have straight A's. But that doesn't mean I like it.

I prepared to stand and walk downstairs when the phone rang. "Now who could that be?" I muttered. I walked to the phone. "Hello."

"Hi, babe," It was Jeremy.

Instantly my face lit up. "Hey, sweets. What's up?"

I was wondering what we were going to do tonight," he asked.

"Well Jeremy, there is a jazz festival going on downtown. How about if we take some food and have a little picnic there," I suggested shyly.

"You want me to eat out of a basket in public," He teased.

"If you're ego can handle it," I teased back.

"With you by my side, I think I can handle that," He said kiddingly.

"Cool, pick me up at eight. I need to finish my book report."

"Does that mean you're getting off of the phone now?" he asked.

"Yep. But you'll be on my mind the whole time," I assured him.

"Good. I'll see you at eight."

I hung up the phone and went downstairs to start my book report.

"So you guys went to the Jazz Festival?" Amity asked.

"Yeah, it was really nice too," I looked at the price tag of the dress I was holding. "We had a good time."

"That's nice," Amity answered. "Hey look at this dress. Isn't it perfect?!"

I looked at the forest green dress. It was ankle length and made from satin. It fell in one long graceful swoop. It reminded me of a very chic slip dress. "It's perfect for you. You have to get it!" I exclaimed.

"Wait," Amity cried. "It costs $250. I can't afford that much. My budget is $200."

"I'm sorry Amity. That sucks," I gave her a shoulder hug. "Maybe we can find one like it for less money. Why don't you try in that section?" I pointed off to the far left.

When I was sure she couldn't see me, I took the dress to the counter. "Excuse me," I said, speaking to the sales clerk. "Is there a way to have this dress delivered?"

"Of course," she answered. "Where do you want it sent?"

I gave her the address, and paid for the dress. I may not have been able to find a dress for myself, but I wasn't going to let Amity pass on the perfect dress for her.

I walked back over to Amity and told her "I hear they're having a larger sale later this week. Let's come back, and see if the dress is on sale okay?"

Amity looked around for a second then slowly said, "Okay."

As we started walking towards the exit, Amity stopped and faced me. "You know its times like this that I really resent my dad. He promised that I would always have anything I wanted," she took a deep breath. "Then he left us. If it wasn't for him, I wouldn't have to scrape together money for the senior activities, plus help Mom out."

"I know, Amity," I gave her a hug. "But don't let him spoil your life."

She pulled away. "That's easy for you to say, at least your dad sends checks each month."

I gave her a long look. "That's true. I replied slowly. "But when it comes down to it, neither one of us has a father that feels we're worth visiting, do we?"

Amity looked at me with tears in her eyes. "No I guess not." I put my arm around her shoulder. "Let's go home."

Chapter Fourteen

"Well, I don't understand. I mean the whole idea behind the Senior Play was to pay a tribute," I looked at Mr. Green seriously. "What will we do if it's cancelled?"

"I honestly don't know," He shrugged his shoulders. "The budget had to be cut suddenly, and the play was the first to go."

"This is just great." I walked towards my locker. I felt as if I had been cheated. Everything had revolved around this stupid play, and now it was going to be cancelled. This was my way to make my official break through back into the normal world. I had the boyfriend, the new clothes, but I wanted to prove that I had the 'strength'. The play would have helped me establish that.

"Hey what's up?" Amity skipped up next to me. Her reddish brown hair was swept up in a ponytail. She wore a white t-shirt with khaki overalls; she dug into her backpack and pulled out a pear. "Did you hear about the play?" She was struggling to keep up with me. "Hey slow down!"

I paused and sighed. "I'm sorry, Amity. Yeah, I heard about the play. What am I going to do now?" I looked into her dark brown eyes. "You know how important this play was to me."

"I know," She answered understandingly. "I honestly don't know what can be done." Her voice turned serious for a second. "Look, I need to talk to you. Are you going straight home after school?"

I thought for a second. "No, I'm supposed to meet Jeremy," I remembered. "Why don't I call you when I get home?"

"It won't be all late will it?" she asked irritably.

"No, I promise. We're just going to go look at some tuxedos."

The bell rang for fifth period. "Okay, I'll talk to you then." Amity turned and walked towards English 402.

"So what about the Mickey Mouse collection?" The sales person asked.

I turned to look at Jeremy's face. He had his arms around my waist. "Well?" I prompted.

"I have always liked Mickey," he admitted.

"Me too," I agreed. "Let's choose that one. My dress is red, so it'll match." I turned all the way around to give him a kiss.

"Just go ahead and reserve this one," Jeremy instructed the salesperson. "I'll call to schedule a fitting later this week."

We walked out of the store and headed towards his car.

"So, straight home?" He asked.

"Yeah," I looked at him regretfully. "Amity said she wanted to talk, and I promised I wouldn't call too late."

"Well, I can respect a girl's promise," Jeremy teased. He bent over and kissed the tip of my nose.

"Thanks for understanding," I took a deep breath preparing to talk. "So we're going to rent a limo with Amity and Daniel, right?"

"Yes," Jeremy shot me an interested look. "I didn't know Amity was exclusively dating Daniel."

"Well, she isn't really," I admitted. "But she does like him a lot. She thinks he would be a good date for the prom. I think so too."

"So you think Daniel might be a good date, huh?" Jeremy asked slyly.

"For *her,* not for me," I assured him.

"Good." He put his arm around my shoulder with a smile. "Very good."

Mom was waiting for me when came home. "Hey Mom what's up?"

"Minah, come sit down, I need to talk to you." Mom was sitting in a chair next to the window; I sat down in the chair across from her.

"What's wrong?"

"Minah, Amity is waiting for you in your room." I stood up immediately. "Minah, sit down," Mom ordered.

I slowly sat down, and looked at her.

Mom sighed. "Minah, Amity has been crying. She says you bought her prom dress for her. Is that true?"

I looked down. "Yeah I did."

"Why did you do that?" Mom asked sadly. "Don't you know that made her feel like a charity case?"

"I didn't think she would take it that way."

Mom laughed an empty laugh. "From the time Amity was a child, she has always had a lot of pride." She paused. "Remember when she was nine, and I took her school shopping with us? There was a jean jacket that you wanted, and I knew she wanted it to, so you guys could match. But when I tried to buy it for her, she got really upset," Mom looked thoughtful. "I will never forget the things she said to me. They really hurt my feelings. She told me that she didn't want any handouts, that she didn't want me to feel sorry for her. She never understood that I was just trying to be kind."

"I had forgotten about that," I admitted slowly.

"Well, she hasn't," Mom assured me. "Now I think you better tell me why you bought that dress."

"Mom, I promise I will," I stood up. "But let me tell Amity first."

I slowly opened the door to my room, and looked in to see Amity laid across the bed reading. I noticed that the dress was laying on the love seat.

"Hi," I said softly.

"I brought the dress back," She said bluntly. "I had wanted tell you that I couldn't afford to pitch in with the limo. That's what I wanted to talk to you about earlier. Then this dress came. So not only can I not afford the limo, but now I have to find a way to cover the cost of a dress that I already told you I couldn't afford." She waved her hand towards the love seat.

"Amity..." I began.

"Dang, Minah. I am not someone that you need to feel sorry for. You know I have the money from my job. I just needed to cut back on some expenses."

"I know, but I wanted you to have a fun prom and not have to worry about not having the perfect dress," I answered.

"Well, that's not going to happen," She said stubbornly.

"Why can't it!" I exclaimed. "My God, Amity. You are the closest thing I have to a sister. You are family. Family does for each other."

"You're right," Amity said with tears in her eyes. "You are so right. But I swear it's so hard."

I walked over to the bed, and put my arm around her. "Then let me make it easier, please," I whispered.

Amity looked at me, and sobs engulfed her, while I held her in a hug.

Chapter Fifteen

"Well, did you decide what you're going to do for your "coming out" to the world?" Amity's voice had a teasing lilt to it.

"I have been thinking about it," I looked at her seriously. I picked up my taco and took a bite. "I don't need it. I have to let it go." I answered with my mouth half full.

Amity turned her head, and her nose crinkled in disgust, "Oh that's so nasty. You could have swallowed your food first *Minah.*"

"Yeah, yeah. But seriously, I was depending on an outside event to prove to everyone else who I am. I need to work on proving who I am to myself first."

"Good for you," Amity agreed.

"So did you ever finish that mural at Sunny Ridge? Amity asked.

"I actually did!" I exclaimed. "I forgot to tell you. It is a field of flowers and butterflies." I smiled. "They want me to work with the residents on another one later in the summer."

"That's really cool Minah. I'm glad you started doing that again," Amity smiled.

"So, about our big night . . . you going to spend the night at my house before we go to Grad Nite?" I asked.

Grad Nite is this totally cool weekend designed for seniors. Ours was taking place at Disneyland, and then we were going to hang around Los Angeles for a few days. It was all organized by the school, and there were even chaperones. But it was still going to be cool.

Amity tipped her head back, and dangled a french fry above her mouth. "Yeah, I'll spend the night." She let the fry drop into her mouth. "That way it'll be easier to leave together the next day. Whose house are the guys staying at?"

"Who knows? They'll probably just meet at the bus," I sighed. "You know how guys are." I took a sip of my soda. "Anything that might encourage them to talk for extended periods of time, and they get uncomfortable."

"I guess you're right," Amity sat straight up, her eyes focused on the door of the cafeteria. "You have to see this."

I turned around in time to see Benjamin carrying a candy apple and some pink flowers. He was headed towards Lisa Konley's table.

"Do you think he's going to ask her to the prom?" I asked excitedly.

"He already has a date for the prom, but they're not serious," Amity reminded me as she leaned closer to get a better view. "Oh my god, I think he's asking her out!"

I struggled to hear the words as they left Ben's mouth. Instead all I could hear was laughter. "What's so funny?" I questioned.

"I don't know." Amity stood up to get the full perspective. "But look at his face."

"Amity where are you going?" I asked anxiously.

But Amity was already on her way towards Lisa's table. "What's going on here?" she demanded loudly.

I didn't need to strain to hear her.

"This is none of your business," Lisa coolly answered her.

"Oh yeah, it is my business," Amity curtly assured her. She pointed to Benjamin. "Do you think it makes you more of a person, to laugh at Ben? It's not like you're all that to be laughing at anyone anyway," she paused and let her glance run smoothly over Lisa. "At least he's captain of the basketball team. What are you *a* captain of, besides the S.N.0.B.S." she let her words drag out slowly.

Benjamin looked at Amity with fire in his eyes. "Amity, what are you doing? I don't need you to come to my rescue."

Amity looked at him with apology. "It was just bugging me the way she was treating you."

"Then let me deal with it," Ben stormed out of the cafeteria, dropping the candy apple and flowers in the garbage.

"Well, well, well," Lisa said slyly. "It looks like someone has a crush on someone else."

Amity looked at her evenly. "He's my friend. At least I don't have to humiliate other people to make myself feel big."

"What do you think you just did?" Lisa asked calmly.

Amity swung on her heels and left the cafeteria. I quickly threw my tray out, and followed her. I knew she would be at her locker and she was.

"May I ask what that was all about?" I asked incredulously.

"You could, but you wouldn't believe it if I told you," Amity had her hands over her eyes.

"Try me," I ordered.

"So what you're trying to say is that you have a crush on Ben?" I was pacing on the grass on the baseball diamond. We had decided to cut study hall, so we could talk.

"Yeah," Amity looked at me expectantly.

"Why didn't you ever say anything?" I stopped pacing and looked at her." Does he know?"

Amity laughed. "Oh yeah he knows."

"Then what's wrong?" I asked reasonably.

"He has reservations about you." She replied bluntly.

"Why?!" I exclaimed. "We never went out."

"And he doesn't think we should, because we're friends."

"But Jeremy and I were friends." I pointed out. Amity looked away. "What?" I asked. "He doesn't approve of it, does he?" I guessed.

Amity shrugged. "He said friends are supposed to be just friends."

"Oh he did, did he?" A thoughtful expression came over my face. "I've known Ben for a long time, and there's more behind that statement, and I'm going to get to the bottom of it."

Chapter Sixteen

"**M**inah, don't take it personal," Ben stopped setting the table and looked at me. "It's just that since we were friends, we have never, none of us, dated people in our group."

"So!" I exclaimed. "We met in elementary school; we're in high school now. We're seniors, for god's sake."

"Why are you so defensive?" He was putting out the silverware.

"I don't know," I sighed and plopped down in a chair. "Maybe because I want you to approve."

"Why?" Ben asked softly.

I stopped and looked at him sadly. "I don't want this to break our friendship apart. Jeremy and I are happy. Very happy. We aren't trying to get married; we're just trying to date. Nothing's wrong with that. But you have this stupid notion that if you date Amity, things will fall apart. Don't you see that it would only bring you closer?"

Ben looked up and ran his hand over his low fade. "I just don't see how."

"Ben, you and Amity have been friends forever. You don't think, even if you did break up, that your friendship wouldn't still last?"

Ben slowly looked at me. "Minah, sometimes I don't know what to think. I don't know …maybe?"

I stood up and walked to the front door. As I opened the door, I glanced back. "You have to figure that out. Nothing personal Ben, but I feel sorry for you." I let the door close behind me.

"So Minah," Amity crooned. "How did it go?"

I had stopped at Amity's house after leaving Ben's, and I wanted to break it to her gently. "I don't know. Got some juice?"

"You know where the refrigerator is," She pointed towards the kitchen.

I started in that direction and Amity followed behind. "So?"

"Girl, Ben is trippin'. For real," I slipped into my "Min-ity". That's the language me and Amity use when we don't want to talk properly (as my mother called it). "I talked to him and it wasn't getting through. For 30 minutes straight we talked. Nada! He just doesn't want to mess the friendship up. Like it will really suffer."

Amity poured some grape juice in a glass and joined me at the kitchen table. "Okay," she said softly. "Now break it down for real."

I closed my eyes and took a deep breath, then opened them again. "Amity, he's scared. I think he really likes you, and he's too frightened to make that step towards you. He really values your friendship," I paused and scratched my head. "But it's not just you. It's the whole gang. He doesn't like that I'm with Jeremy, but he's only said it to you and me, not him. I don't understand him."

Amity propped her elbows on the table and put her head in her hands. Slowly she looked up with a sad smile. "So what are we going to do about it?"

I called Jeremy that night and explained my plan to him. It was brilliant. We were going to get Ben and Amity in a situation where they are forced to talk alone. I was going to invite everyone over to my house and then create some way for them to run an errand together. Even if it takes several tries, I know it will work!

"Minah are you sure you want to involve yourself in this?" He sounded worried.

I sighed. "I don't want to be, but I need to be for everyone's sake. We aren't first graders, we're twelfth graders, and things have to change!"

"You're right." He agreed. "So, we start tomorrow?"

"Tomorrow," I repeated.

As soon as I hung up the phone with Jeremy, Mom called me for dinner.

"Sit down, eat with me." Mom patted the seat cushion and smiled.

"Hi Mom." I bent down and gave her a kiss.

"I haven't seen you for fifteen minutes today. As soon as you got here, you took off in your car." She looked curious.

"It's just teenage drama," I explained. "Benjamin refuses to recognize that we aren't children anymore, and its okay to date our friends. He thinks it will ruin our friendship."

"Minah, but you are children," Mom argued.

"No, we're teenagers, there's a difference," I pointed out.

"I guess there's a little difference. Who does Ben want to date?"

"Amity," I bit into my steak and rolled my eyes. "She likes him too, but *he's* scared to mess up the friendship."

"Poor Ben," Mom responded.

"Poor Ben?" I exclaimed. "What about poor Amity?'

"Amity?" Mom scoffed. "Amity just stopped talking to Daniel. She just broke up with Justin. Amity is on the move."

"But, Mom." I leaned back in my chair. "I think this time she's serious."

Chapter Seventeen

"Tonight for homework, design an original recipe based on the principles of chemistry," Mr. Collins stood at the front of the room behind his desk. "Turn last night's homework in at my desk on the way out. You're dismissed."

"So do you want to work together tonight?" Anthony asked me. He put his baseball cap back on his head. Hats were not allowed in Mr. Collin' room. "You know, two heads better than one'?"

"I'll do you one better," I said thinking. "Amity and Ben have this class seventh period. Four heads could be even better." And make my plan go into action.

"Great. About 5:00?" He asked.

"You need a ride?" I asked.

"No, I'll hitch with Ben." Anthony stopped by my locker as I got my English things out. We hadn't planned it, but we had the majority of our classes together. But that was cool. Out of all the guys, I had always had the most in common with Anthony. His tall, thin frame stood next to me as I went through my locker.

"Minah, what's up with Ben lately?" Anthony's voice was unusually serious. He reached down and straightened his boots. I put my things in my bag, closed my locker and started towards English.

"I really thought I would ask you that. That's your boy," I said.

"Me?" Anthony squeaked. He touched his chest. "I know nothing. Ben hasn't played ball all week. That's when we do most of our talking."

As we reached English class I stopped. "Ant, Ben just wants something and he doesn't know how to get it. We have to help him. He has feelings for Amity."

"Serious?" Anthony asked shocked. "I had no idea. That's cool."

"He doesn't think so," I explained our earlier conversation.

"But I have a plan. You in?" I asked.

Anthony smiled. "No doubt."

"Well, we know that bread has yeast in it," Ben stated.

"That's obvious," I cried out exasperated.

We, meaning Amity, Ben, Anthony, and I were spread out on the family room floor. I had invited Jeremy, but he had a book report due the next day.

"I think we should try to bake it or broil it," Amity suggested, half serious.

"Yeah right," Ben rolled his eyes. *"Can you even broil bread?"*

"What are you saying?" Amity asked in a low voice.

"Anthony, did you see the preview for the new sci-fi movie?" I asked quickly.

Anthony took the cue. "I love sci-fi, we have to see it, guys."

"Of course we will." Ben looked at Anthony soberly.

For forty-five minutes, we had managed to keep the discussion on Science. Finally, we were ready for a snack. I was actually starving, and the others agreed. It was time to eat.

"Who wants to order pizza?" I asked. Mom had left money because every Thursday, she worked late. I was used to getting my own dinner.

"Pizza sounds great. We'd better pick it up," Ben suggested. "It's cheaper that way."

"Who wants to get it?" I asked. Anthony made a move, but stopped when he saw my eyes on him.

"I'll go," said Amity. She tossed her hair into a ponytail and stood up.

"Not by yourself," I objected. "And I need to stay here. Ben, you mind?"

He looked at me with pure evil in his eyes, but when he looked back at Amity his eyes softened. He thought no one noticed, but I saw it right off. "Sure. I'll go."

I tossed him my keys and smiled. "Take my car."

As Anthony and I finished up our recipe, Ben and Amity left for the pizza.

"Hey Anthony," I gleamed. "Step one of my plan is underway."

As they got into the car Amity thought heavily. "I don't want to be here," she thought. "I don't want to be here."

Ben was equally heavy in thought. "I don't want to mess anything up. I don't want to mess up anything up."

He started the car and they headed towards Round Table. A memory surfaced inside him, and he laughed. "Hey Amity, remember when Lavendar used to order pizza for Minah's dinner, and Minah would call us and make us hide in her room?"

"Yeah," Amity chimed. "Then she would sneak up pizza to us. Lavendar always wondered how she ate so much."

"Yeah," Ben took a deep breath. "That was fun. We had a lot of fun times together."

"We still do," Amity reminded him.

"But soon we'll all be at college. It'll be different," Ben's voice was sad.

Amity looked at him closely. In his black jeans and green Polo shirt, he looked harmless enough. She was used to seeing him casual, but most of the girls at school would have had to look twice to recognize "Designer Ben". He always dressed in the latest fashions. That's why he and Lavendar got along so well. Ben wanted to design men's casual wear, although he would rather die than admit it.

"Ben, we're all going to be in Atlanta. It'll be cool. We always have each others' backs. You know that," Amity reached over and touched his free hand.

Ben briefly looked at her. "Yeah."

They pulled into Round Table and placed their order, then settled into a booth. They had at least a twenty- minute wait.

"What will you major in?' Amity asked.

"I think Business Management," Ben looked at her thoughtfully. "That way I could open up my own store. Like Eddie Bauer or Sean John.

"Hey, then I could get a discount on stuff for my boy-friends," she teased.

"Of course." Ben said sarcastically.

"Hey Ben, I was only joking," Amity sobered up.

Ben shook his head. "I'm sorry Am, I'm just preoccupied."

"Ben, I know what's going on," Amity said.

But while she was talking, Ben was finding it hard to concentrate. Amity had her hair in a loose ponytail pulled to the side. She wore a pair of loose fitting blue jeans, and a purple sweatshirt, and she looked great. Like himself, Amity had a variety of stylish clothes, but somehow the group always got along better when they were just casual.

"So I guess what I'm saying is that...I understand," Amity had finished her speech and Ben had missed all of it. Ben looked confused. "I'm sorry Amity, what?"

"You didn't hear a word I said!" Amity exclaimed. "What were you doing?"

Ben lost all pretenses and simply said, "I was looking at you."

"What?" Amity was shocked and it seemed a little strange.

Ben took her hand in his own. "Tell me, just how stupid have I been?"

Amity looked towards the pick -up counter, turned back, and answered. "The pizza's done."

Chapter Eighteen

"That's all you said?" I questioned. I was on the phone with Amity, and I was trying to get the full story.

"What did you want me to say?" Amity said exasperated. "I've already risked too much."

I started to brush my hair. I was actually ready for bed, and dressed for it in Mickey Mouse boxer shorts, and a T-shirt. "I don't know. Something like 'I think you've been very stupid, but I still like you?'"

"You're too romantic," she huffed.

"Well, one of us has to be," I pulled my hair into a ponytail and hit the lights. "I'm going to bed, 'night Amity."

"'Night Minah."

The weekend was here, and the possibilities were endless. I could either hang out with Amity, hang out with Jeremy, or veg out on the couch. I slipped into a pair of sweats and headed towards the couch. I started flipping through the channels and settled on a re-run of Family Ties. I love that show.

About 3 hours had passed when the phone rang. "Hello." My mouth was half full of pretzels.

"Minah," Ben sounded confused.

"Yes, Benjamin, it's me," I swallowed the pretzels. "What's up?"

"Can I come over?" he sounded kind of down.

"Ben, you know you never have to ask," I replied softly. "Come on."

I had unlocked the door after Ben called, so he could walk straight in. He sat down in a chair opposite from the couch where I was still vegging.

Ben looked at me. " I need to talk to someone, and I don't think any of the guys could truly understand. Besides Amity," he looked pained as he said the name, "you're my best girl friend."

"Ben, save the drama." I sat up and looked at him honestly. "You've been acting like a jerk. You offended me and Jeremy, and you insulted Amity. But we all love you, so we can overlook it."

"She told you what happened didn't she?" He frowned.

"Yeah, she told me." I waved my hand in front of him. "And excuse me, but what kind of line is "tell me how stupid have I been?""

Ben shrugged and said nothing. I tried to look at him objectively. Ben was attractive. He had dark brown hair, the same color eyes, and all the makings of the athlete he was. He was captain of the basketball team, and he had also played football, but with the seasons being over, these days he just lifted weights.

"Ben, you don't know what you did." I walked over and knelt in front of the chair. "Amity really likes you, and you found the lamest excuse not to go out with her."

Ben looked at me with tears in his eyes. "I do know

what I did, and I want to make it better. I just don't know how to make the transition. I like her so much, and she's my best friend. How do you do that?" Ben dropped his head." Will you help me?"

I reached up and hugged him. "Of course I will," I whispered.

I should probably explain that Ben's dad left Ben's mom about two years ago. No one really understood why, after twenty-eight years of marriage. Ben is an only child, and he and his dad were very close. The last thing Ben remembers about the goodbye is overhearing his dad tell Ben's mom that he didn't want what they had anymore. Ben always thought that also meant him being his son. In a way, I guess it does. Ben can do the dating thing fine, but when it comes to a serious relationship that involves trust, that presents the problem, a very large problem.

Because my father left us, I can somewhat understand. Of course my dad left after my mom had me, and they were never married. My dad comes around every once in awhile. He's an attorney, and he makes very good money. I'm lucky, I have everything I want. But who minds having a Dad? My dad wasn't always an absentee. When I was first born he still lived with us. He and mom were a struggling couple. Mom had her modeling gigs and Dad had just finished law school. Mom told me they started fighting over money first, then they just started fighting over everything. Dad decided to leave and mom was fine with that. They agreed to share custody of me. Dad would pick me up on the weekends, and that worked for awhile, but when he finally got a job, his firm wanted him to travel. Weekend visits turned into monthly visits. Soon, I was seeing him just for my birthday and holidays. Slowly the visits stopped altogether though he did call now and then. Mom always said she understood, and raised me not to hold it against him. He just wasn't ready to be a dad. But when she started her business and it grew, she still had time for me. It's hard not to resent my dad, but I can't live my life waiting for him to focus on me. I still love him, and I do have Mom, I have my friends, and I have me. That will do for now.

Chapter Nineteen

*I*t really wasn't my place to butt in. I knew that, but Ben and Amity were getting nowhere. It had been a full week, and Ben was still moping around, and Amity was through with trying to act like she didn't care. I hated to see it, and I knew that all they needed was someone to help them talk their feelings out. That person would be me, of course.

I picked up the phone and dialed Amity's number. "Come over in about half an hour," I demanded.

I did the same thing to Ben, and then started the preparations to what I hoped would be an effective meeting.

I walked back to the phone, and called Jeremy. After hearing my idea, he felt it would be beneficial if he was also there. That way Ben and Amity could see an example of friends turned boyfriend and girlfriend.

I sat on the couch and waited for my friends to arrive. I

started thinking about the time in grade school when Amity and I got into our first major fight. It was Ben that got us talking again. I kinda felt like I owed it to him. The shrill sound of the phone jerked me from my thoughts. I reached over and picked it up. "Hello," I answered.

"Hello," the deep voice responded.

"Daddy?" I asked, surprised.

"Who else has a voice this deep?" he joked.

He had me there. My dad's voice is almost as deep as that guy's from The Temptations. "What's up?" I was really happy to hear from him. The last time I saw my dad was three months ago, when he came to San Jose on business.

"Nothing's up," He answered. "I thought I would call my little girl. How's everything with you?"

"I miss you," I said softly. "Other than that, everything's good." I talked about school and all my end of year plans. "I have a new boyfriend," I said.

"So who's the lucky guy?" He asked sternly.

"You remember Jeremy?" I asked.

"The new guy?" he responded.

"Yeah, well we got together. He's really sweet," I assured him.

"He better be." My dad got silent. "Listen, Minah is your mom around?"

Now that was a surprise. Mom and Dad were not on the best of terms. They always kept me out of it, but still, it was no secret.

"Yeah, she's upstairs. Hold on. I love you Dad," I replied.

"I love you too," Dad said softly. Just then the doorbell rang.

"Mom, telephone!" I yelled, then ran to the door and opened it to find Amity standing there. "Hey girl." I guided her inside. "Want anything to drink?" The doorbell rang again. "I'll be back."

I left Amity standing there, and ran back to the door. This time it was Jeremy. "Hey sweets." I kissed his cheek.

"Hey kid." Jeremy hugged me close.

"We're not alone, Jeremy." I said quickly.

"Hey Jeremy." Amity sang out.

"What's up?" Jeremy walked over and gave her a hug. And just then wouldn't you know, the doorbell rang again.

"Hey Minah," Amity said. "You having a party or something?"

"Or something." I opened the door to see Anthony. "Hey, what are you doing here?" I asked, shocked.

"Minah, you invited the whole gang over, and left me out. Don't you think we should all be part of this little meeting?" Ant almost looked sad.

"Of course." I gave him a hug. "Sorry."

"Am I missing something?" Ben was in the open doorway. I looked at him hard.

"Nope, you're right on time."

Chapter Twenty

We were all sitting around the room. I was in my customary seat, sprawled out on part of the couch, Amity had the other end. Ben was in the recliner, and Jeremy and Anthony were on the floor.

"So, seriously Minah, what is this all about?" Ben asked.

"I know that this may seem drastic, but we really need to have a group discussion," I paused and looked at Jeremy. "You haven't been with us that long. In that time we haven't had one of these, but it's a tradition. Whenever a problem occurs that concerns all of us, we meet until we can solve it. I already let my mom know that it might take awhile, and she agreed to send for Chinese," I looked at my watch. "So we have all day."

"So," Amity breathed heavily. "Let's start." She looked directly at Benjamin.

"Good idea," Anthony agreed. He focused his green eyes on Amity. "Why don't you begin? What problems are you having with Ben?"

Ben looked around. "No offense, but I am not doing this with all of you here. Get lost for just a few seconds, okay?"

We looked at each other. "Come on Jeremy and Ant. We can go in the kitchen," I said.

"That was too personal," Amity objected as she watched us walk out.

"Yeah so personal that even I don't know what it's about," Ben scoffed.

"You would if you tried being honest with me," Amity argued, turning to look at him. "Why is it so hard for you to admit that you like me? And don't try that friend thing. Look at Amity and Jeremy. They've been together for over a month. They're still friends."

"Please," Ben hooted. "Jeremy is not a good comparison to me."

"What's that supposed to mean?" Amity asked.

Ben held his hand up. "Amity, we have known each other since we were six. Jeremy and Minah met a few months ago."

"True," Amity conceded. "But you even have a problem with them."

"It doesn't really have to do with them," Ben disagreed. "I just thought that friends shouldn't mix. You trust your friends, more than your girlfriends anyway." He looked away.

"Ben," Amity looked at him shocked. "Is that what you think? That if I became your girlfriend, you wouldn't be able to trust me?"

Ben looked at her. "I don't know," He answered honestly.

"Ben, I'm your best friend. I love you. If you can't trust

me, who can you trust?" Amity folded her arms. "We're all best friends. We all love each other. We all have trust. Don't ever doubt that." She looked worried and troubled. Ben was quiet for a while.

"So what do you think?" Amity asked." Are you we going to try it or not?"

"Amity?" Ben walked over to the couch. "I have come to understand that my feelings have changed for you. I like you as more than a friend." He picked up her hand. "Will you go out with me?"

Amity leaned over and kissed his cheek softly. "Ben, I was just waiting for you."

"Think we should let them back in?" Ben asked after giving her a hug.

"Sure why not." Amity said happily. "Minah, you guys can come back now!"

"Great," I announced, running into the room. I searched Amity's face for a clue. She smiled and Ben smiled with her.

"Anthony, call Tiana, and invite her over." I looked at Jeremy beaming. "We're having group date night."

Jeremy leaned over and kissed me softly. "And tell her we're having Chinese."

Lavendar appeared in the archway. "Did someone say Chinese?"

Chapter Twenty-One

*A*fter getting everything cleared up, things could only get better. Or so you would think; but I remembered my dad telling me once, "Things have to get worse before they can get better".

"Now students, please remember Senior or not, you must pass your remaining classes with a grade of C or better, or you will not graduate," Principal Victor was speaking at the annual Senior Prep Assembly. Otherwise known as the 'This is Your Last Chance' Assembly. We all knew that if your grades weren't up to par at this point, graduation was not likely.

"Why does he always wait so long to say that?" Amity whispered. Even though we weren't at the assembly last year because we were only juniors, Principal Victor's speech was notorious. *Everyone* had it memorized long before senior year.

I shrugged, and glanced at Ben who just looked at me and shrugged back. I leaned towards Amity; "It's almost over now. He'll say, 'Of course I don't anticipate a problem out of this bunch'."

"Of course I don't anticipate a problem out of this bunch," Principal Victor announced.

We both dissolved in laughter until Mrs. Lewis caught my eye. I nudged Amity, "Cool it. Lewis is watching."

Amity sobered up, and muttered, "I can't wait until graduation".

"One large pepperoni and black olive pizza and five cokes. That all?" The waitress passed out plates and headed towards the next table. We were at Round Table all crowded into a booth going over the final details for the Senior Ball. The Ball was next weekend, and everything had to be perfect.

"Okay, I'll stop at Minah's first with the limo and pick her up," Jeremy paused and thought for a minute. "We should probably head towards Amity's next, they're close by. So Ant, you'll be the last one. That cool?"

"Hey, as long as I get to go to the Ball, I'm cool," Anthony was smiling as he said it, but his eyes look worried.

"What do you mean? You are going, aren't you?" I asked.

Anthony smoothed down his blue T-shirt and rubbed his arms. "Hopefully. I mean yeah."

"Oh Lord," Ben rolled his eyes." What is it now?"

"I refuse to be the object of pity," Anthony protested.

"Well do you prefer to watch us go to the Ball?" Amity countered.

"I have a D in Math," Anthony admitted quietly. "I have to pass the final with a B in order to pass the class."

"How long have you known?" Ben asked.

"About 2 weeks," Anthony looked up.

"Of course," Ben answered. "Of course you've known for 2 weeks and have said nothing to anyone. Did you think not saying anything would make it go away?"

"No . . ."Anthony started.

"You do realize that the Ball is not the real issue? Graduating is. College is. My God, what have you been doing?" Ben's voice had risen considerably.

"Excuse me. But who do you think you are? Last time I looked dude, you were not my father." Anthony stood up. "Get off my back."

Ben scooted over and also stood up. "Anthony, man, come on. I am just trying to help. I'm just surprised, man."

"Get out of my face, man," Anthony threatened.

"Ant c'mon, don't go there. We're boys." Ben reached out.

Anthony shrunk back. "Correction, we used to be boys." He stalked away angrily.

"What was that all about Ben?" Amity exclaimed. "I mean dang, you came down hard."

"So what," Ben turned towards Amity. "Ant's been screwing around. He got accepted to a good school, and he got lazy. We're supposed to be going to Morehouse re-member? We didn't work this hard to fail."

"Man, it's not your problem." Jeremy responded." You can't make him pass."

"Yeah it is." Ben argued. "Anthony came up from a D student to an A student just so he could get accepted to Morehouse. So we could go together. I'm not going to let him fail!"

"Ben, yelling's not going to help." Amity put her hand on his arm.

"Amity, mind your own business." Ben pulled away.

"Anthony's my friend, so that makes it my business." She looked at Ben hard. "And I thought you were my busi-ness too. I guess I was wrong. Excuse me, Minah."

I stood up to let her out. I watched her walk out the same way Anthony had a few minutes earlier. Our party of five had turned to a party of three.

"I thought we were all boys," Jeremy said. "Fighting is not going to help, we need to support each other."

"Oh my God!" I exclaimed. "Can't we just stop? You all need to just sit down together and talk all this out."

"Minah, please. Don't try to fix this." Ben stood up. "Just leave things alone. This is between Anthony and me."

"Benjamin. We are all friends." I patted the seat next to me. "Sit down; let's find a way to help Anthony pass."

"Minah!" Ben yelled exasperated. "Why do you always have to be Ms. Fix-it? I'm out." He headed towards the exit.

Silently I watched him walk out. I turned to look at Jeremy. "What's going on?" I wondered sadly.

Jeremy shrugged. "Wish I knew. We just gotta stay out of it."

"I wish it were that easy," I said running my hands over my hair. "I feel useless, helpless. I mean everyone's mad. Senior Ball is in two weeks. Everything is falling apart." I looked at him. "The whole night will be ruined.'

Jeremy looked at me unbelievingly. "I can't believe this. Your best friend may not graduate and you're worried about the Senior Ball?" He stood up. "Grow up, Minah."

I saw Jeremy leave, looked around the empty booth, and caught my reflection in the mirror. And then there was one.

Chapter Twenty-Two

I was in my room reading a book when the phone rang. "Hello." I answered.

"Hi," Jeremy's reluctant voice replied.

"What's up?" I asked coolly.

"Babe, I'm sorry about last night," Jeremy apologized. He sighed. "There just seems to be so much tension."

I turned over on my side. "Yeah. I know. I talked to Amity this morning. She and Ben still aren't speaking. I know I was all about the Ball, but Jeremy, seriously, I care about my friends a lot more."

"Minah, I know you do," He paused. "So should we even try to fix this?"

"I think not," I answered quickly. My feelings were still hurt by Ben's words. "For once I'm staying out of it."

"I don't blame you,." He agreed. "But how are things going to stand?"

I stretched my arms above my head, and looked at the ceiling. "I honestly don't know."

"The purpose of this last meeting is to choose the 'Friends' that will represent the graduating class."

Each year the graduating class nominated a group of friends that seemed the closest of that year. Mrs. Jennes was introducing the senior goodbye theme during our last class meeting.

"When choosing the friends, we look for those of you who have over the last year been consistent, loyal, and sincere in your friendship." Mrs. Jennes looked out at us all and smiled. "And how do we know who those friends are? Ladies and gentlemen, believe it or not, your teachers do notice things, and sometimes they even talk about them," She giggled. "And when that doesn't work, we ask you. This group was nominated by your senior class officers."

Mrs. Jennes glanced at her sheet and raised her head. "Before announcing our Senior Class Friends. Let me first list the responsibilities that these young people will have. First, they must attend all senior events together. Second, they must have at least a 3.0 average at the end of finals, and they must create a namesake for the future Senior Friends. That is produce memorabilia marking this event."

Mrs. Jennes took off her glasses and her face lit up. "The Senior Friends for this year are: Amity Phillips, Minah Steele, Jeremy Smith, Benjamin Waters, and Anthony Washington."

I sat straight up. "Oh my God." I looked over at Amity and we both screamed. We threw out arms around each other, and we were almost knocked down when Anthony came running over to us. Jeremy reached through Amity and Ant, and pulled me into his arms. When I turned around Ben was standing there. He looked at all of us sheepishly. "Get over here silly," I cried.

Mrs. Jennes voice came over the microphone. "Could

this year's Senior Friends please come on stage?"

"Minah, you talk," They all said in unison.

I didn't even complain, I felt so happy.

We all climbed the stage steps and crowded around the microphone. I stepped up. "First, I want to say thank you. This is an important day for many reasons," I paused and looked back at my friends. "We've been arguing a lot lately. You see, we're all going our separate ways very soon, and we're still getting used to that. I think I speak for all of us when I say we're scared."

The audience laughed nervously. "I guess we're all scared," I observed. "But we'll be fine. I'm lucky. My friends are like family to me, and we'll all be in Atlanta, at different schools, some of us, but at least all in the same city. We can't afford to let little things come between us. Time goes by too quickly."

Again, I turned around and looked at my friends.

"I used to think that making friends was easy," I looked back at the audience. "And it is, but making *and* keeping true friends is hard. You have to work at it, and you have to love the people you hang with."

Amity stepped up next to me and put her arm around my shoulder. "You have to be willing to admit when you're wrong."

Anthony stepped up next to Amity. "You have to admit when you need help."

Ben stepped forward. He glanced at Amity. "You have to admit when you care. Oh and by the way, Lisa Konley, I got someone so I'm not sweatin' you no mo'!" He smoothed his over-sized sweatshirt down, and stepped over to Amity.

"But the biggest thing..." Jeremy started as he stood next to me. "... is you have to be willing to love." He stood squarely in front of the mic. "Many of you know that I am new here, and the first person I met was Anthony, at the gym. Who knew all these great people would come with him?"

The audience laughed.

"But," Jeremy continued. "It's a package deal. When you get one you get us all. True dat?" He looked at us.

We looked at each other, smiled, and said in unison, "True dat!"

Chapter Twenty-Three

The last two weeks of school sped by. Benjamin agreed to tutor Anthony, and he got a B on his final; and of course the extra credit Anthony piled on didn't hurt either. As Senior Friends, we stayed busy hanging out and representing the class by going to all the senior events. We had already planned to go together anyway, so this was just icing on the cake. Graduation was very emotional. It was an end of an era, but one that we would always hold close to our hearts. All of our parents came to see us go through our rite of passage, and even my Dad came. Will wonders never cease?

Amity and Ben continued to get closer, and they were truly a couple now. Jeremy started hanging out at my house more, and he and Mom began to get tight. Amity and I spent time just doing "girl" things, and preparing for college.

Did I mention that we were all going to school in Atlanta? We had already decided to try to go to school in the same city, and we all were accepted to colleges in Atlanta. I was going to Spelman, Benjamin and Anthony were headed to Morehouse, and Amity and Jeremy were attending Clark. With Jeremy being from Georgia, we were excited to see what the south was like.

So, you have truly witnessed my metamorphosis from a caterpillar to a butterfly. Would I recommend that all girls go through this? Not hardly, but I hope you did learn from my mistakes and from my successes. Hey, I had a few! What I hope you really learned was how valuable your friends are. Without my friends, who knows what my senior year would have been like? I would have spent a lot of time alone, and very unhappy. Benjamin, Anthony, Jeremy, and Amity are priceless gifts. I love my friends, and I am looking forward to seeing what adventures we get into while we're at college. You're interested too? Well, that's another story.

Printed in the United States
145889LV00002B/1/P

9 781432 722357